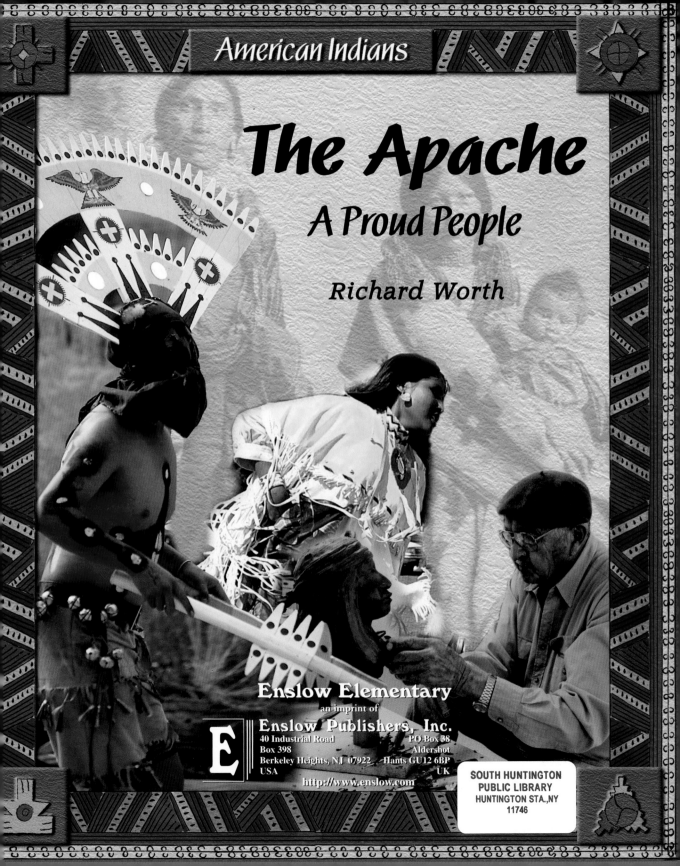

The Apache

A Proud People

Richard Worth

Enslow Elementary
an imprint of

Enslow Publishers, Inc.
40 Industrial Road   PO Box 38
Box 398   Aldershot
Berkeley Heights, NJ 07922 Hants GU12 6BP
USA   UK

http://www.enslow.com

Editor's Note: *We at Enslow Publishers, Inc., are aware that the people of the nation described in this book call themselves N'de. However, since they are still often known as the Apache, we have decided to use this term. We mean no disrespect to the N'de people, but just wish to reach as many readers as possible in order to tell the rich history and current accomplishments of this vibrant people.*

Enslow Elementary, an imprint of Enslow Publishers, Inc.

Enslow Elementary® is a registered trademark of Enslow Publishers, Inc.

Copyright © 2005 by Richard Worth

Library of Congress Cataloging-in-Publication Data

Worth, Richard.
    The Apache: a proud people/Richard Worth.
       p. cm.—(American Indians)
    Includes bibliographical references and index.
    ISBN 0-7660-2415-6
    1. Apache Indians—History. 2. Apache Indians—Social life and customs. I. Title.
II. American Indians (Berkeley Heights, N.J.)
E99.A6W68 2005
979.004'9725—dc22

2004008047

To Our Readers: We have done our best to make sure all Internet addresses in this book were active and appropriate when we went to press. However, the author and the publisher have no control over and assume no liability for the material available on those Internet sites or on other Web sites they may link to. Any comments or suggestions can be sent by e-mail to comments@enslow.com or to the address on the back cover.

Illustration Credits: AP/Wide World Photos, pp. 1 (girl), 4, 23, 27, 43; Clipart.com, pp. 12, 34; Colorado Historical Society, pp. 13 (bottom), 30; © Corel Corporation, pp. 6, 17, 22; Denver Public Library, Western History Collection, pp. 10, 39; Enslow Publishers, Inc., p. 7; Hemera Technologies, Inc., pp. 13 (top), 14; Lee Marmon, pp. 1 (sculptor), 41; © Marilyn "Angel" Wynn, courtesy of Nativestock.com, pp. 1 (dancer), 11, 21, 29, 31, 33; North Wind Picture Archives, pp. 35, 36; Photos.com, p. 26; Reproduced from the Collections of the Library of Congress, pp. 1, (background), 10 (inset), 15, 18, 19, 37, 40; Sun Valley Photography, courtesy of Nativestock.com, p. 32; U.S. Fish and Wildlife Service, p. 25.

Cover Illustration: AP/Wide World Photos (girl); Lee Marmon (sculptor); Marilyn "Angel" Wynn, courtesy of Nativestock.com (dancer); reproduced from the Collections of the Library of Congress (background photo).

Contents

Kevin Dakota Duncan performs the hoop dance at a contest in Phoenix, Arizona.

Children of the Earth and Sky

In the past, the old men of the Apache tribe told stories to the children. As they listened, the children chewed on corn kernels. One of these stories explained the beginning of the world. The sky was a man, called Father. The earth was a woman, called Mother. She looked up, and he looked down. They were the parents of the Apache.

The Apache created a successful way of life in the Southwest. Most Apache families hunted and fished. The land helped shape Apache beliefs. For a long time, the Apache moved freely across their lands. However, white settlers tried to end the Apache way of life. They killed the Apache and drove them away. The Apache resisted and gained the right to live on large pieces of land called reservations.

As of the year 2000, almost one hundred thousand Apache lived in the United States. As that number continues to grow, the Apache celebrate the lasting tradition of their people.

❖ chapter one ❖

The Land

The Apache were often on the move. They eventually settled in what is today the American Southwest.

The Apache Then

Thousands of years ago there was a land bridge connecting Asia to America. At that time, the ancestors of the Apache, the Athapascans, crossed over the bridge. They settled on land now part of Alaska and Canada.

Between A.D. 1000 and A.D. 1300, the Apache moved southward. They settled in present-day Arizona, New Mexico, and Texas.

The Apache lived in different groups. The Jicarilla Apache settled near the Rio

Much of the Apache land is covered with brush and cacti.

The Apache once lived throughout the Southwest. Today, there is land on which only the Apache can live. This land is organized into reservations. The colored areas represent the original Apache lands.

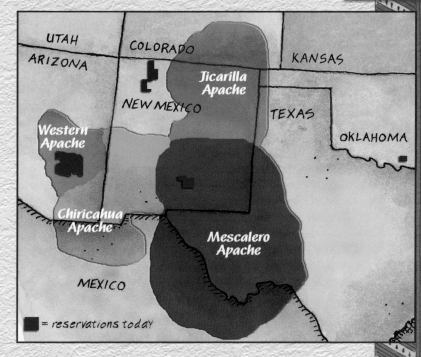

UTAH
ARIZONA
COLORADO
KANSAS
NEW MEXICO
Jicarilla Apache
TEXAS
OKLAHOMA
Western Apache
Chiricahua Apache
Mescalero Apache
MEXICO
■ = reservations today

Grande River in the mountains of northern New Mexico. The Mescalero Apache made their home in the southern New Mexico desert. The Chiricahua Apache moved to the mountains and deserts of southern Arizona and New Mexico. The Western Apache lived in central Arizona. The Lipan Apache could be found in Texas.

The Apache Today

Today, many Apache are still in these areas. They live on reservations in Arizona, New Mexico, and Oklahoma. They also live in other places throughout the country.

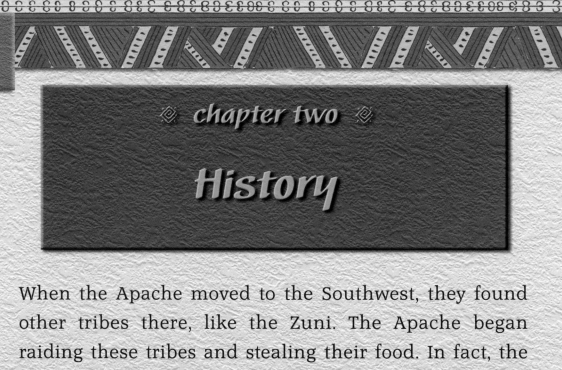

chapter two

History

When the Apache moved to the Southwest, they found other tribes there, like the Zuni. The Apache began raiding these tribes and stealing their food. In fact, the Zuni may have first used the name "Apache." It means "enemy." The Apache call themselves "N'de." It means "the people."

In the 1500s, the Spanish arrived in the Southwest. From the Spanish, the Apache learned to ride horses. The

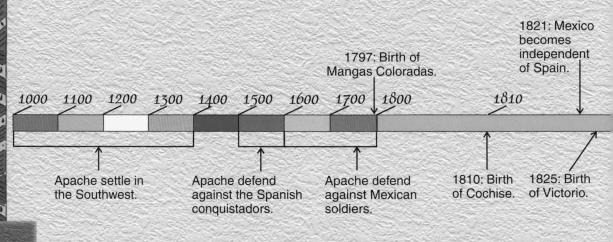

1797: Birth of Mangas Coloradas.

1821: Mexico becomes independent of Spain.

1000 1100 1200 1300 1400 1500 1600 1700 1800 1810

Apache settle in the Southwest.

Apache defend against the Spanish conquistadors.

Apache defend against Mexican soldiers.

1810: Birth of Cochise.

1825: Birth of Victorio.

Spanish invaded the Apache lands from Mexico. Battles continued for the next three hundred years. During the 1800s, Mexico became independent from Spain. After a war with the United States, Mexico was forced to give up large areas in the Southwest.

American settlers gradually moved into the Southwest. They began to set up farms on lands on which the Apache lived and hunted. New wars broke out between the Apache and the United States Army. The Apache were led by great chiefs. They included Mangas Coloradas, Cochise, Victorio, and Geronimo.

By the 1880s, the Apache were moved from their villages to reservations. Most of them live there today. Some Apache also live in large cities.

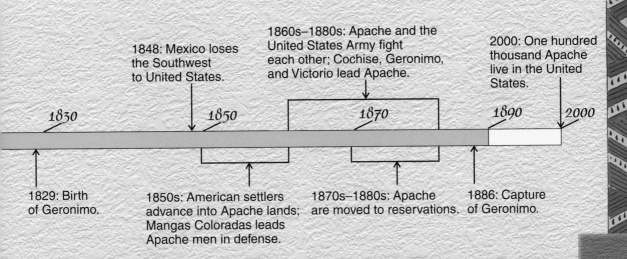

1848: Mexico loses the Southwest to United States.

1860s–1880s: Apache and the United States Army fight each other; Cochise, Geronimo, and Victorio lead Apache.

2000: One hundred thousand Apache live in the United States.

1830   1850   1870   1890   2000

1829: Birth of Geronimo.

1850s: American settlers advance into Apache lands; Mangas Coloradas leads Apache men in defense.

1870s–1880s: Apache are moved to reservations.

1886: Capture of Geronimo.

chapter three

Homes

The Apache hunted animals that moved from place to place. They needed homes that could be built and taken apart easily. Modern Apache need strong, safe homes.

The Apache Then

Some Apache, like the Lipan, lived in tipis. These were homes shaped like triangles. They were made from poles stuck into the ground. The poles were tied together at the top. They were then covered with buffalo hides.

An Apache woman and girl build a wickiup (inset).
A medicine man and his family sit in a wickiup.

Many of the Apache lived in wickiups. They were made from wooden poles placed in holes in the shape of a circle. The poles were lashed together at the top. Over the poles, the Apache laid heavy grass in the warm weather and animal skins in cold weather. A hole remained at the top so the smoke could escape from a fire.

The Apache Today

During the 1900s, the Apache built wooden cabins on the reservations. Today, they live in houses made of brick, cement, and other modern building materials. However, the Apache still use wickiups at special events.

These modern Apache homes are in Arizona.

chapter four

Clothing

Apache clothing was made from animal hides. Today, their clothing has changed, but many Apache keep tradition alive.

The Apache Then

Apache men hunted deer, elk, and buffalo. Women used knives to remove any hair from the hides of these animals. The hides were softened by rubbing them with warm animal brains. Afterward, each hide was allowed to dry until it became soft leather buckskin. Sometimes the buckskin was painted with colorful designs.

Men often wore buckskin breechcloths. A flap in the front

This Apache man is dressed for the winter.

was attached to a belt, tucked between the legs and hooked to the belt in back. To stay warm, men also put on buckskin shirts and ponchos. Women wore skirts with fringe at the bottom as well as buckskin ponchos.

Both men and women wore moccasins on their feet. Some Apache wore low moccasins. Many others had knee-high moccasins.

The Apache Today

In the early 1900s, Apache began wearing western-style clothing. However, they still put on traditional clothing for special ceremonies.

Moccasins protected the feet of the Apache.

This woman's skirt is made from buckskin. It is decorated with beads.

chapter five
Food and Meals

The Apache lived off the land. Today they still respect nature and rarely waste the food they find or buy.

The Apache Then

The Apache rarely grew crops. Instead, Apache women gathered fruits and nuts during the year. In spring, they cut the stems from yucca. These are large plants with white flowers. The Apache dried the stems for food.

In summer, wild berries grew in the Apache lands. Women gathered currants, wild raspberries, and strawberries. These were often dried to preserve them for the winter when no berries grew. The Apache gathered wild onions, potatoes, and various

Strawberries were and still are part of the Apache diet.

kinds of nuts. These included acorns from oak trees and piñon nuts from pine trees.

The Apache mixed nuts and vegetables together with meat to form stews. Men hunted deer, elk, and antelope. As early as the 1500s, the Apache obtained horses from Spanish explorers and began hunting buffalo.

Another Apache food was mescal, from the agave plant. The mescal was cut, then baked for a day. This created an important food for winter. The Mescalero Apache were named after mescal.

The Apache Today

Today, the Apache buy food from grocery stores. However, they also make the recipes of their ancestors, like acorn stew.

Two Apache women prepare a meal in 1903.

chapter six

Family Life

The Apache people lived together in large families. Both historic and modern Apache have realized the great importance of family life.

The Apache Then

Families included grandparents, parents, cousins, aunts, and uncles. Each married couple had their own wickiup. Every family had a headman or leader who made sure that all important work was done.

Sometimes a number of large families would build their wickiups next to each other. They lived together in a group. These families might gather or hunt for food together in the summer. The men might go on raids against other tribes.

Young people in Apache society were expected to marry. Girls married while they were still in their teens. However, boys were usually older.

Young men and women might meet each other at a dance. Later, a boy could show he was interested in a girl. He might leave some animal meat, which he had killed, at her wickiup. She would show her interest by cooking the meat and giving some of it to him.

Marriages had to be approved by the couple's parents. Both sets of parents gave each other gifts. These might include horses or blankets. The Apache did not have a formal marriage celebration. Generally, a man went to live with his wife in a wickiup close to her parents. He became part of her family, and their children became part of her large family group.

Married couples did not believe in showing their love for each other

A young Apache man would often hunt deer or other game and give the meat to a girl he liked.

Ed Ladd poses with his family in 1886.

in public. They only kissed in private, inside their own wickiup.

The Apache had a strict rule. A man was never supposed to look at his mother-in-law. They believed that this action helped prevent problems in marriages.

When a couple had a child, a medicine man said some prayers. These prayers were meant to help protect the baby.

After the birth of a child, a woman carried her baby in a cradle board. This was made of wood, curved at the sides. Strips of rawhide were stretched over the wood to hold the baby. A wooden covering protected the head of the baby. A mother could put the cradle board on her back to carry and protect the baby while she was working.

The Apache Today

Today, Apache families have close ties between grandparents, parents, and children. Instead of relying on medicine men, most Apache women rely on doctors or nurses to help them give birth. However, some Apache women still use cradle boards.

A mother holds her baby in its cradleboard.

chapter seven
Everyday Life of Children

Children learned what it was to be an Apache at an early age. Today, they still take part in certain ceremonies.

The Apache Then

Apache boys and girls had to pass certain tests before they became adults. When they were still children, boys had to learn to swim and run fast. These activities helped to build their strength.

From Apache warriors, boys learned how to make bows and arrows as well as spears and clubs. These weapons were used in hunting. A boy had to show that he was a good hunter before he was considered a man.

A boy also had to learn how to live in the wilderness. He had to know how to hide from wild animals and outsmart his enemies. Apache men took their sons on raids against other tribes. They were expected to show their bravery in these battles. Once they passed these tests, the boys became men.

Girls had similar tests. They had to build up their strength through running and swimming. They also had to learn how to cook, sew, and hunt for nuts and berries.

Before a girl became a woman, she had to go through the Sunrise Ceremony. The Apache believed that the ceremony was begun many centuries earlier by White Painted Woman—an important Apache spirit.

Apache boys learned how to use the bow and arrow. They would also use a war club (foreground).

At sunrise, a wickiup was built for the girl who was the center of the ceremony.

The ceremony lasted four days. It began before sunrise on the first day. The young girl, who played the part of White Painted Woman, wore a skirt and a poncho painted yellow. She had a decorated, wooden cane and wore an eagle feather in her hair. A wickiup was built just for her at sunrise.

On the first day, the girl danced and songs were sung about White Painted Woman. The girl was massaged by her godmother. This was done to make the girl strong so she could do the work of a woman. She was also blessed with pollen from flowers. That night, dancing occurred. It was supposed to remove any sickness from the girl.

Over the next few days, there were prayers and singing.

Each night dancers wearing masks performed at the ceremony. On the last day, the wickiup was taken down. Gifts were thrown into the air for the children. The girl went back to her parents' wickiup. She had become a woman.

The Apache Today

Today, Apache boys are not taught warfare, but they are sometimes taught to hunt. A few Apache girls still go through the Sunrise Ceremony. Their family finds a camping place and builds wickiups. Then they participate in the ceremony for several days.

Claudia Griggs runs around a cane during her Sunrise Dance. The cane was made by a medicine man.

chapter eight

Religion and Medicine

Religion was an important part of everyday life. Today, Apache have more than one religion from which to choose.

The Apache Then

The Apache believed that the sun, the moon, the lakes, and the mountains were spirits. The Apache prayed to these spirits daily for help in hunting and other activities. According to Apache beliefs, one of the most important spirits was Child of Water. He was the son of White Painted Woman. The Apache believed that Child of Water killed the monsters of the world so it was safe for people to live on Earth.

The Apache feared that evil spirits lived in the world. Some of them were the ghosts of people who had died. The Apache were afraid of death and buried a person who had died far away from their villages. The dead

person's wickiup and all of his or her belongings were also destroyed.

However, the ghosts of the dead might return at night. The Apache believed that these ghosts often lived inside owls. The Apache feared the hoot of an owl, which might mean death.

The Apache also believed in witches. Many witches were men. These men might bring illness to an Apache by shooting objects into them. They might be pieces of hair, small pieces of wood, or tiny pebbles. A witch might also cast a magic spell on someone to bring evil on him or her.

To remove the sickness, the Apache asked for help

The Apache believed that ghosts lived in owls. This pygmy owl lives in New Mexico.

Shamans used pollen from flowers to heal the sick. In this picture, the pollen is the yellow powder.

from a shaman, a medicine man or woman. They believed that shamans could control the power of the spirit world. They could use this power to heal illness.

Pollen from a flower was often used in curing illness. The sick person would put pollen on the shaman, and he would rub it on his patient. The shaman was often followed by dancers. They would beat their drums and dance for several nights as the shaman sang.

Sometimes an illness was believed to be caused by a witch. The shaman would find the pebble or piece of wood that the witch had shot at his victim. Then the shaman would spit the object out into the fire to remove the illness.

During the past two centuries, the Apache mixed their traditional beliefs with new ones. Priests and ministers brought the Christian religion to the Apache.

The Apache Today

Today, most Apache people are Christians. Doctors and nurses replaced the shamans. However, old Apache men and women still believe in the shaman's power.

Hollis M. Chough waves a feather and recites an American Indian prayer in Scottsdale, Arizona. He does this to honor the Apache leader Victorio and his men.

chapter nine

Arts and Music

The Apache have always made time for arts and music in their daily lives.

The Apache Then

The Apache were gifted storytellers. Some of these stories described the way the world was made. Others told of powerful spirits that lived in the mountains. They were called Gan and could bring good or evil. Apache dancers wore painted masks that looked like the faces of the Gan at some of their ceremonies.

These colorful masks were among the many types of crafts created by the Apache. Women also made baskets. These were woven together from thin strips of wood. The strips were cut from willow and cottonwood trees. Apache women also decorated the baskets with stripes, designs, and pictures of animals. They took great pride in their skills as artists.

Baskets were very important for the Apache. They used them to gather berries and nuts. Some baskets were covered with pitch so they could hold water and would not leak. The pitch came from the piñon pine tree. Other baskets were used to store food after it was gathered, so it could be used during the winter.

Apache women also wove trays. These were used to serve food. Women made plates from wood and bowls from gourds. Some Apache tribes created pottery that was gray and black.

Apache women were skilled at decorating clothing. Skirts, dresses, and shirts had bold designs of dancers, wickiups, and desert animals.

This dancer performs at the group celebration in New Mexico.

This basket was used to carry water. Pictures of a horse and rider were painted with natural brown dye.

Apache men used their skills to make weapons. From the wood of an oak or locust tree, they made bows. These were three or four feet long, painted, and decorated with colorful designs.

Some of the most beautiful craftsmanship went into head-dresses worn by Apache warriors. Some headdresses were decorated with beads. They had feathers and horns from animals.

Apache warriors also made shields from the hides of buffalo and other animals. They were often decorated with eagle feathers. The Apache used these weapons in battle as well as in tribal ceremonies.

The Apache held many ceremonies throughout the year. Some of the ceremonies were meant to bring rain to the dry desert. The Apache celebrated when a wickiup was built. Shamans also used ceremonies to cure the sick. These ceremonies included dancing, chants, and drum music.

The Apache Today

Today, traditional music is still played at Apache ceremonies. The Apache also make colorful baskets and other handicrafts. These are often sold to tourists on Apache reservations.

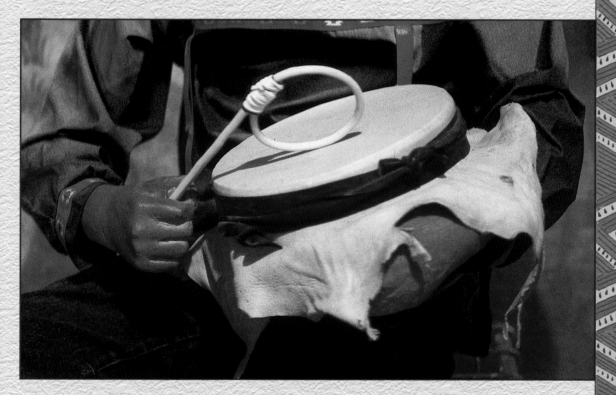

The drum is one of the many musical instruments that the Apache play.

chapter ten

Sports and Games

Although there was much hard work to be done, the Apache still found time to have some fun.

The Apache Then

One of the favorite Apache games was a relay race. The fastest runners in a village challenged another village to a race. Each man could run one part of the race or more. The winner was decided when one team was so far ahead that the other could not catch up.

Another popular Apache game was hoop and pole. In one version of the game, a mound of hay was placed in a field, and a narrow opening was made through

A group of Apache play hoop and pole in 1899.

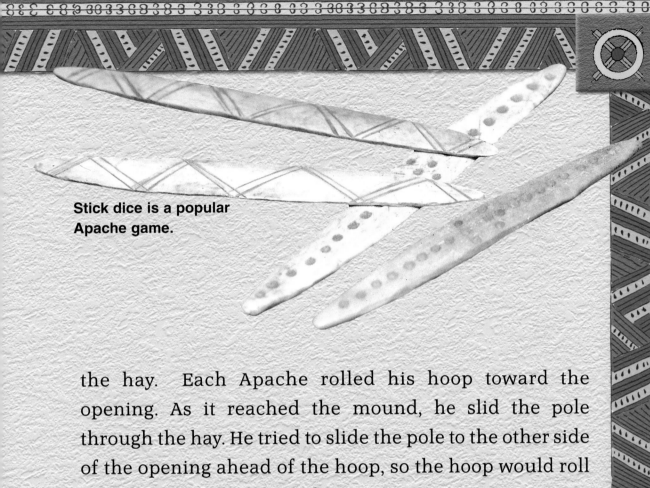

Stick dice is a popular Apache game.

the hay. Each Apache rolled his hoop toward the opening. As it reached the mound, he slid the pole through the hay. He tried to slide the pole to the other side of the opening ahead of the hoop, so the hoop would roll through the end of the pole.

Women enjoyed a game played with stick dice. These were flat on one side and rounded on the other. Three dice were thrown against a flat rock. Scores were made by how many dice landed on the flat or rounded sides.

The Apache Today

Today, the Apache still enjoy many games. They play baseball and basketball. Some Apache also compete as rodeo riders.

chapter eleven

Warfare

After the Apache came to the Southwest, they sometimes raided other American Indians. They were later forced to defend themselves from the United States Army. Today, they are a peaceful people.

The Apache Then

During the 1540s, the Apache met some Spanish soldiers. The soldiers were led by explorer Francisco Vasquez de Coronado. The Spanish soldiers were looking for rich cities filled with gold and silver, but never found them.

Coronado (top left) and his men watch the buffalo of the southwest.

Father Juan Padilla tried to convert American Indians to Christianity during the 1500s.

The Spaniards brought horses to the Southwest. The Apache learned to ride horses. The Spaniards captured some of the Apache and used them as slaves on their farms. As a result, wars between the Spanish and Apache broke out that lasted for the next 250 years.

Meanwhile, Spanish priests were trying to win over the Apache to Christianity. Sometimes, they destroyed Apache religious masks and tried to stop them from praying to their spirits. This upset the Apache. They attacked Spanish settlements.

In 1821, Mexico became independent of Spain. However, the wars against the Apache continued. From 1820 to 1835, the Apache killed or captured about five thousand Mexicans. They also attacked American traders who were coming to the Southwest. In 1837, a trader named James Johnson invited the Apache leader Juan

Jose into his camp and promised him food for his people. Once Juan Jose arrived, he was killed.

After defeating Mexico in the Mexican War, the United States took control of the Southwest, including the area where the Apache lived, in 1848.

During the 1850s, Americans traveled to the Southwest looking for gold. To protect them, the United States Army sent more soldiers and built forts.

New Mexico Governor James Calhoun signed a peace treaty with the Jicarilla and Mescalero Apache. However, Congress did not approve the treaty.

During the mid-to-late 1800s, the United States cavalry killed many Apache so settlers could take over Apache land.

For the next twenty years, the Apache attacked wagon trains of settlers coming west. But the Apache had less men than the American soldiers. In 1871, General George Crook took over command of the soldiers in the Southwest. He hired

Geronimo and the Apache meet with General Crook and his cavalrymen in 1886.

some American Indian scouts to help him fight the Apache and their leader Geronimo. Gradually, Geronimo and his men were defeated.

The Apache Today

The Apache fought in World War I, World War II, and the Vietnam War. A monument in Lawrence, Kansas, called "Comrade in Mourning," honors the Apache killed in World War II. However, the Apache no longer use warfare to solve their problems with the American government. They rely on the courts and talks with political leaders.

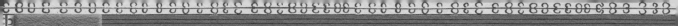

chapter twelve ✦

Heroes

The Apache heroes excel in many areas of life.

The Apache Then

Several Apache heroes led the fight against the Americans, whom the Indians called "white eyes." One of them was a chief of the Chiricahua Apache, Mangas Coloradas. He was born in southern New Mexico about 1797. Coloradas was a large man, over six feet tall. In 1837, Mexican trappers massacred many Indians. Coloradas led the tribes in a war against Mexico.

After the United States took over the area in the 1850s, Coloradas tried to become a friend of the Americans. But gold miners killed some of the Apache. Coloradas asked the miners to leave, but they whipped him. Coloradas led his people on the warpath for the next ten years. He was finally captured by the U.S. Army in 1863 and shot.

Another leader among the Apache was Cochise. He was born about 1810. During the 1850s, Cochise became a war chief of the Chiricahua Apache. At first, he tried to make friends with Americans. But in 1861 he was accused of kidnapping a white child. Cochise was invited to the camp of Lieutenant George Bascom. When Bascom tried to arrest him, Cochise cut a hole in the tent and escaped from the camp.

War broke out between Cochise and the American soldiers. However, the Apache were outnumbered. Eventually, Cochise decided to make peace and agreed to live on a reservation. He died in 1874.

A third Apache leader was Victorio. He was born in southern New Mexico about 1825. During his twenties, he participated in raids against Mexican settlers. In 1860, a group of miners attacked a peaceful Apache village. Victorio and his men began raiding

Chief Victorio (1825–1880) was a great Apache leader.

In 1906, Geronimo stands over the last buffalo that he hunted.

American settlements in the Rio Grande Valley of southern New Mexico. In 1880, he was trapped in the Tres Castillos Mountains of Mexico by U.S. and Mexican troops. Victorio and most of his warriors were killed.

The death of Victorio still left the Apache chief Geronimo on the warpath. Geronimo was born about 1829 in Arizona. He was a shaman with many followers. Geronimo continued raiding settlements until the 1870s. Then he led his warriors onto a reservation.

Geronimo did not like reservation life. Over the next ten years, he escaped, was recaptured, and escaped again. Finally, he surrendered in 1886. He died on a reservation at Fort Sill, Oklahoma, in 1909.

The Apache Today

Among modern Apache heroes is Allan Houser, a sculptor. He was born in 1914, and his parents were

Chiricahua Apache. He is the great grandson of Mangas Coloradas. Houser went to art school in Santa Fe, New Mexico, and later taught students there.

He made large American Indian statues in metal, stone, and wood. One of them, called "Offering to the Great Spirit," is located in New York City. His sculptures celebrate the great traditions of the Apache.

Houser also influenced other successful American Indian artists. They include sculptors like Doug Hyde and Bill Prokopiof. Another well-known Apache is the artist Sharon Skolnick. She is also a writer.

Allan Houser works on a statue of a fellow Apache. This type of statue, which includes only the head, is called a bust.

chapter thirteen

Government

The Apache's form of government differs from that of the United States.

The Apache Then

In the past, Apache camps and villages were made up of several families. They formed a local group that was led by a local chief. He might be a great warrior or a shaman. The chief often lived in a larger wickiup than other Apache. He ran the group with the help of a council, made up of the men who headed each family. He continued to be the chief as long as he made good decisions.

Sometimes, Apache groups were threatened by their enemies. Then they might gather together in a band for greater strength. A band might include three hundred Apache. Each band was led by a chief, like Cochise or Geronimo. He was usually an effective speaker who could win over the other Apache. Before making a decision, the chief asked advice from his council, which was made up of the chiefs of the Apache groups.

The Apache Today

Today the Apache still have tribal councils. They are elected by those living on the reservations. The councils run local affairs, like schools and health care. The tribal councils also deal directly with state governments and the United States government in Washington, D.C., regarding Apache affairs.

A. Paul Ortega (with medal) was president of the Mescalero Apache in 1998.

A Bright Future

The Apache enjoyed their way of life. It was difficult for them to give up the freedom to roam the deserts and mountains to live on reservations. However, today they work toward a better life for all Apache people.

Today the Apache are one of the largest American Indian tribes. Children attend schools on the reservation. They learn English and the traditional Apache language.

Their parents have a variety of jobs. Some work in the lumber industry. Some Apache are employed on cattle ranches. The Jicarilla Apache receive money from the oil and natural gas on their reservation in northern New Mexico. They also have large sheep herds. The Apache make traditional crafts to sell to tourists and to celebrate their past.

Some of the Apache have left to live outside the reservations. They work as teachers, doctors, and lawyers. Wherever the Apache live, they take pride in their history and work to build a bright future.

Words to Know

breechcloth—A piece of clothing for men, worn much like shorts.

buckskin—A softened animal hide.

ceremony—A special event; sometimes religious.

fringe—An edge on clothing made of thin strips of cloth.

gourd—A type of squash that is often hollowed out and dried to make bowls or musical instruments.

headdress—A covering for the head with special decorations.

massage—To use one's hands to soothe tense muscles in a person's body.

medicine man—A religious leader who also helps cure the sick.

moccasin—A soft leather shoe.

pollen—A fine dust on plants that is carried by some insects to other plants so that they may reproduce.

poncho—A sleeveless garment with a hole for a person's head to go through.

raid—To attack with the purpose of gaining food, money, or items.

shaman—*See* medicine man.

spirit—A ghost or some other being which is not part of the physical world.

More Books!

Birchfield, D.L. *Apache*. Milwaukee: Gareth Stevens Publishers, 2003.

Bishop, Amanda, and Bobbie Kalman. *Nations of the Southwest*. New York: Crabtree Publishing Co., 2003.

Corwin, Judith Hoffman. *Native American Crafts of California, the Great Basin, and the Southwest*. New York: Franklin Watts, 2002.

Holt-Goldsmith, Diane. *Apache Rodeo*. New York: Holiday House, 1995.

Philip, Neil. *Earth Always Endures: Native American Poems*. New York: Viking, 1996.

Riordan, James. *The Songs My Paddle Sings*. London: Pavilion Books, 1998.

Stanley, George Edward. *Geronimo: Young Warrior*. New York: Aladdin Paperbacks, 2001.

Internet Addresses

Apache Creation Story

<http://www.indians.org/welker/creation.htm>

PurpleHawk's Nest

Apache information site

<http://www.impurplehawk.com/easy.html>

Southwest Native Americans

Art, Food, Religion, Children, Vocabulary, and Legends

<http://inkido.indiana.edu/w310work/romac/swest.htm>

Index